AlphaFete

A Caribbean Carnival From A to Z

By:
Justina Predelus

Library of Congress Cataloging-in-Publication Data:

Author Name: Predelus, Justina

Title: AlphaFete

Description: First Edition | Miami, Florida: Noir Mien Publishing | Audience 3-7 Identifiers: LCCN 2021906505 | ISBN: 978-1-7361208-7-3 (paperback) | ISBN: 978-1-7361208-8-0 (hardcover) | ISBN: 978-1-7361208-9-7(eBook)

Subjects: Children's Fiction - Juvenile Literature

Category: Juvenile Fiction > Holidays & Celebrations > Juvenile Fiction > Concepts > Alphabet

Website: https://www.noiremien.com/Justinatells

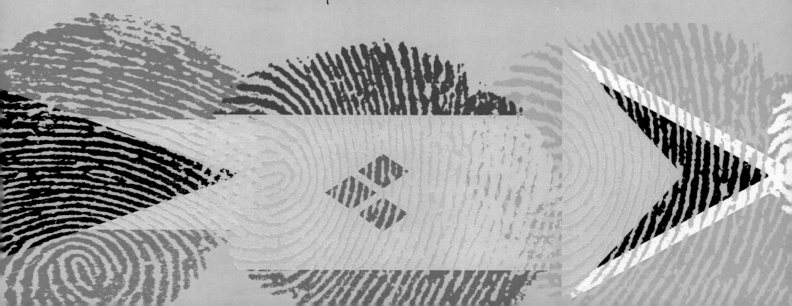

"This book is a celebration of culture and pride, no matter where you are from. Peace, love, and unity is the number one priority for survival. With freedom, we can achieve everything. With strength, we can conquer all... and it can all be done with a smile."

1

You are officially invited to this AlphaFete. Where you can dance, play, and sing, and learn your alphabet. From colorful costumes, face paint, and beautiful hair, find a Caribbean carnival and join a fete there. A fete is a party as most would say. Every country has fetes on its own special days. There is so much to learn from where it all began, but "freedom" is a term you will hear time again. Folklore and traditions make this a yearly celebration. If you choose an island to fete, oh what a lovely vacation. Join us now! What are you waiting for? Now, you will see another day when you will never ever get bored.

Aa

**Allison
Ate
Ackee**

4

Bb

**Bajans
Bend
Back**

5

Cc

**Caribbean
Carnival
Countries**

Dd

**Dominicans
Dance
Different**

Ee

Everyone
Enjoy
Evenings

Ff

Fry

Fish

Fete

Gg

Grenadian
Girls
Glitter

Hh

**Haitians
Have
History**

I i

Island
I
Indies

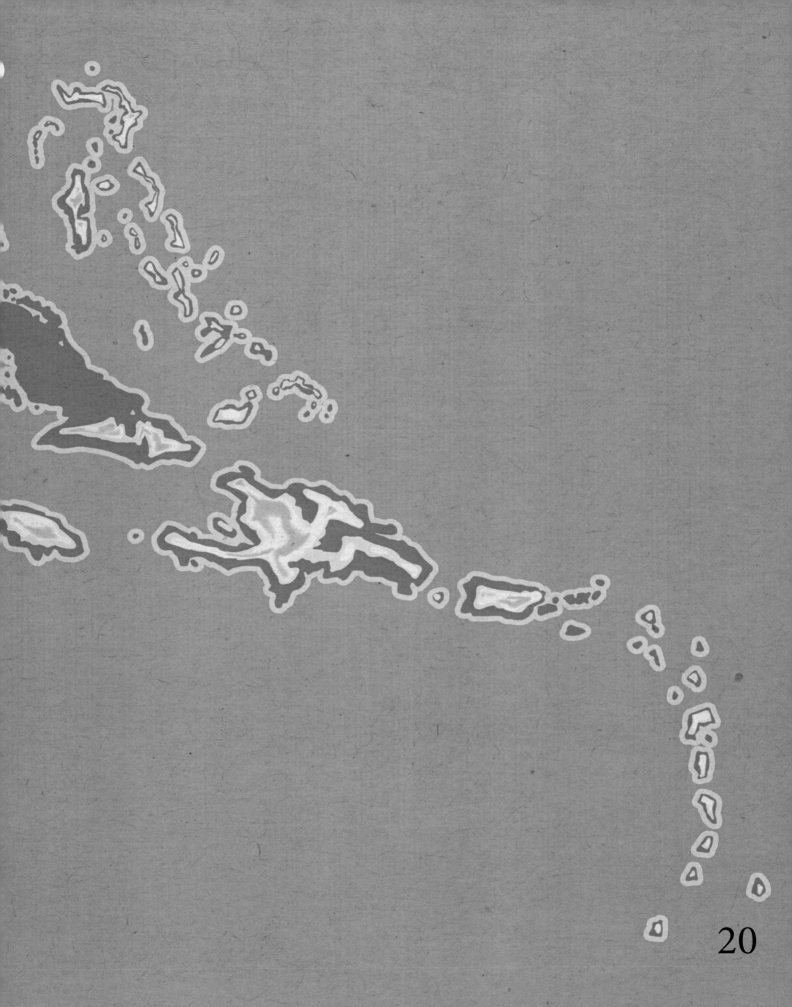

20

Jj

**Jamaicans
Jam
J'ouvert**

Kk

Kindred
Keep
Kitchens

23

Live
Love
Laugh

25

Mm

Machel
Mashup
Mad

28

Nn

No
Naps
Needed

Oo

**Oxtail
Over
Okra**

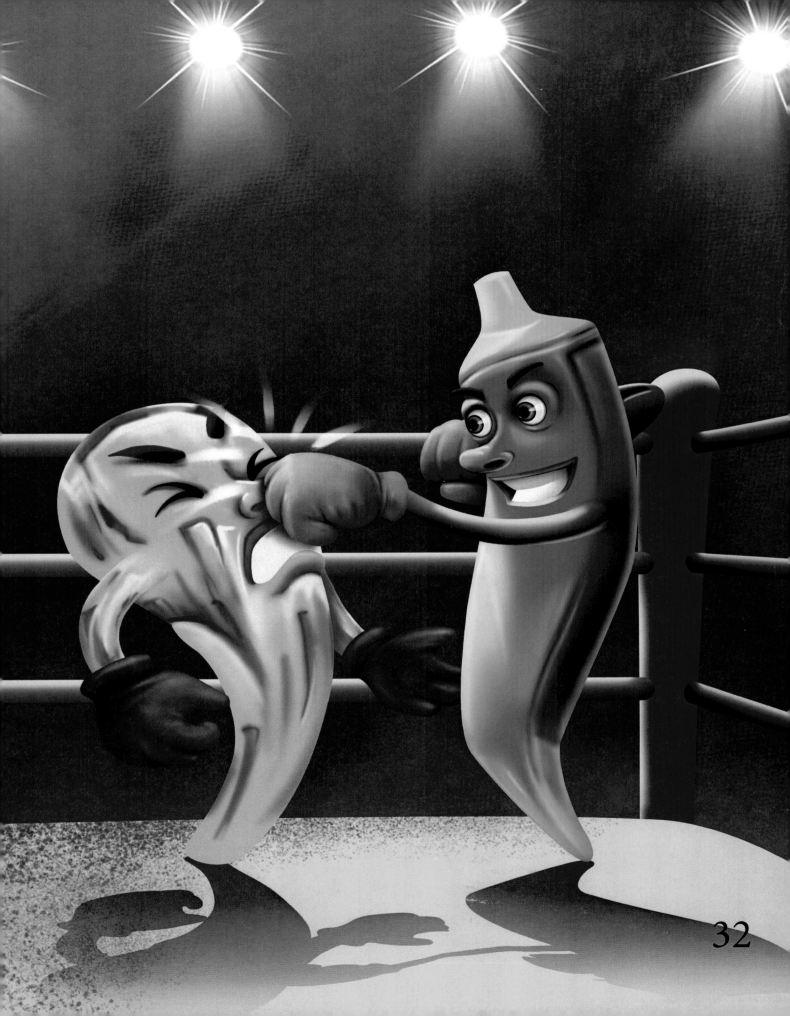

Pp

**Puerto Rican
People
Pride**

Qq

Queens
Quake
Quickly

36

Rr

**Revelers
Run
Roads**

Ss

Soca
Songs
Stilts

39

Tt

Trini
Try
Takeover

42

Uu

Unity
Uplifts
Us

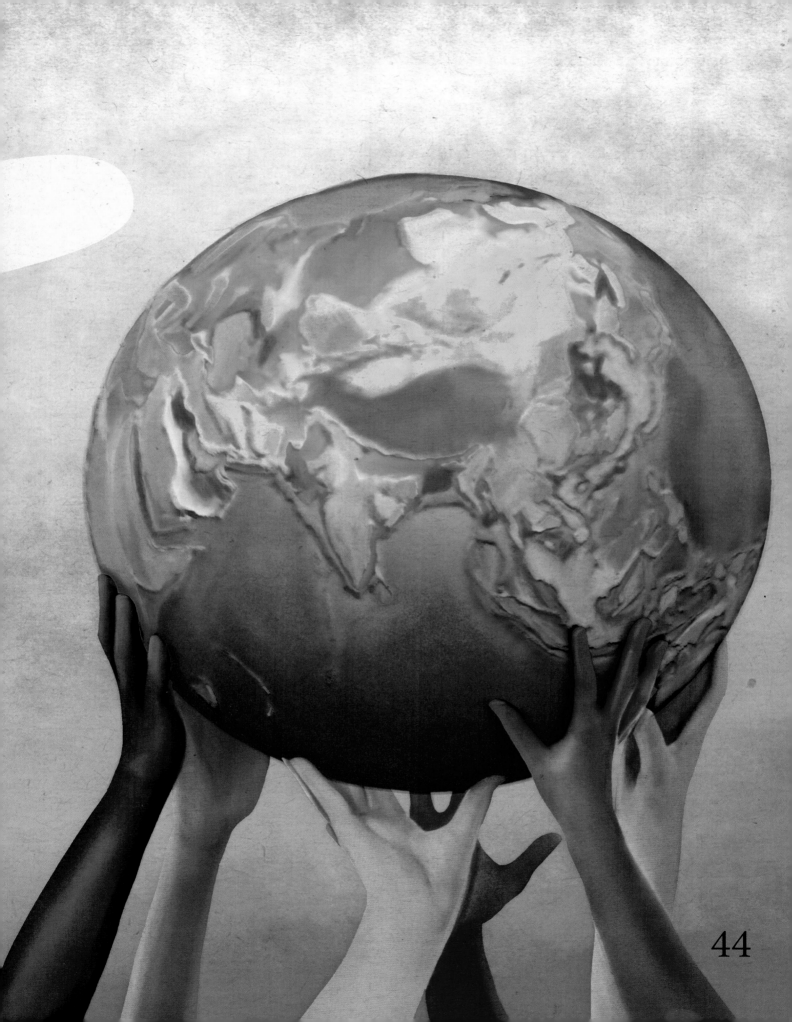

44

Vv

Virgin Islands
Vacation
Vibes

Ww

Waist

Wine

Wars

47

Xx

Xray
Xeno
Xylophones

49

Yy

Yes
You
Year

Zz

Zip
Zen
Zzzzzzz

This is

not...

the

end!

Grab a mic and let us sing!

"AlphaFete" Song Lyrics

A, B, C... D, E, F, G...
H, I, J, K...L, M, N, O, P...
Q, R, S and T, U, V...
W, X, and Y and Z

Thank you, Mama!
Thank you, Papa!
Thank you, Mama!
Thank you, Papa!

Allison **a**te all the **a**ckee.
Bajan girl **b**end it **b**ack.
Caribbean **c**arnival **c**ountry,
Dominican yet **d**ance **d**ifferent.
Bring yourself and **e**njoy the **e**vening.
I gon' **f**ry some **f**ish at the **f**ete.
The **G**renadian **g**irls like **g**litter.
My **H**aitians' **h**istory.

A, B, C... D, E, F, G...
H, I, J, K...L, M, N, O, P...
Q, R, S and T, U, V...
W, X, and Y and Z

Thank you, Mama!
Thank you, Papa!
Thank you, Mama!
Thank you, Papa!

On the **i**sland **I** in the **I**ndies.
Jamaican **j**am **J**'ouvert.
Kindred **k**eep up the **k**itchen,
to **l**ive, **l**ove, and **l**augh.

Machel **m**ash up the **m**ad hey
No **n**aps **n**eeded yet.
Oxtail **o**ver the **o**kra.
Puerto Rican **p**eople **p**ride.
ABCs...I know my ABCs.
ABCs...I know my ABCs.

Thank you, Mama!
Thank you, Papa!
Thank you, Mama!
Thank you, Papa!

We love Soca.
Build us a nation.

Q is for all the **q**ueen there,
R, are you on the **r**oad?
And I like **S**oca, make me feel fine,
The **T**rini **t**ry to **t**akeover,
Unity...it **u**plifts **u**s,
Yea that **V**irgin Island **v**acation,
we a go feel the **v**ibe.

Waist
X..Ray
Yes

Thank you, Mama!
Thank you, Papa!
Thank you, Mama!
Thank you, Papa!

Alphafete!
Come join the Alphafete!
Alphafete!
We at the Alphafete!

About Justina:

Justina Predelus was born and raised in Miami, Dade County. Her parents were born in Haiti and left in search for a better life. She pursued her career in English Education with an Associate of Arts degree and later graduated from Georgia State University with a Bachelor of Arts in English. Justina grew up in the library system, often frequenting weekend and summer breaks at her mother's job. Reading became an adventure to her, and she mastered the creative art of writing. You can travel the world through her inspiring lense as a travel blogger, or you can have a seat in her imagination, but be prepared to never want to leave. Her love for reading and writing has led her down a literary path to success. Join her on her journey as a published author and a blogger at https://www.noiremien.com.

Check out other books by the author!

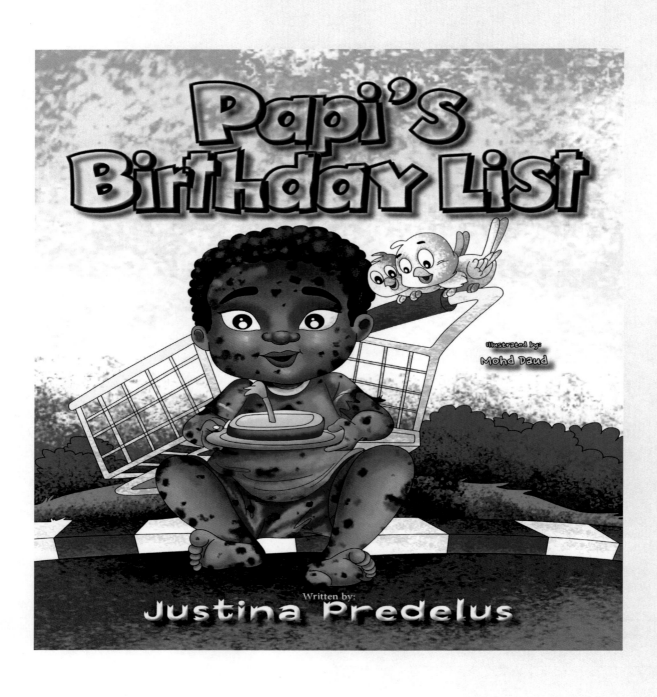

Made in United States
North Haven, CT
19 April 2023

35619579R00042